The Ancient One

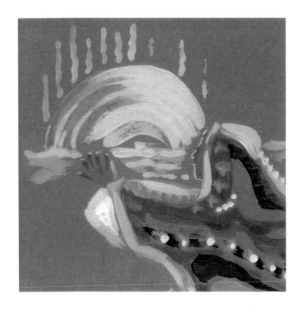

She Was, She Is, She Will Be Always

Sharon Mick McAuley

Artis🌊ns NOrth

Frankfort, Michigan

2011

The Ancient One: She Was, She Is, She Will Be Always
© 2011 Sharon Mick McAuley

"The Ancient One"/ "Little As You Are" CD Recording
© 2011 Sharon Mick McAuley

Subjects for cataloguing and related research:
• the feminine divine
• creation-centered spirituality
• art spirit
• meditation and creativity
• servant leadership
• wisdom traditions
• the ancients
• spiritual formation

ISBN 978-0-615-49353-4

Printed by Infinity Graphics, Okemos, Michigan
www.infinitygraphics.com

The Ancient One

Contents

For

My Great-Grandmothers:

Flora, Jeanetta, Alice, and Delilah

Grandmothers Ruth and Stella

Mother Ruth

Mother-in-law Dorothy

Blood Sisters, Soul Sisters, Global Sisters

Women of Wisdom, All

Wisdom, the fashioner of all things,
taught me.
There is in her a spirit that is intelligent, holy,
unique, manifold, subtle,
mobile, clear, unpolluted,
distinct, invulnerable, loving the good, keen,
irresistible, beneficent, humane,
steadfast, sure, free from anxiety,
all-powerful, overseeing all,
and penetrating through all ...
For she is a breath of the power of God ...
She is more beautiful than the sun,
and excels every constellation of the stars.
Compared with the light
she is found to be superior ...

Wisdom of Solomon 7:22-23a, 25a, 29 NRSV

In her hands

she carries nothing,
fingers free,
wide open palms;

1

On her face

the glow of morning,

night-shade contours

blessing dawn.

On her shoulders

many-colored

woven shawl

of hand-spun yarns,

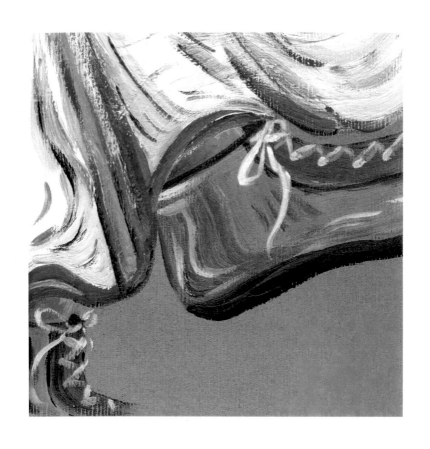

On her feet
soft woolen slippers,
sturdy fit
for walking far.

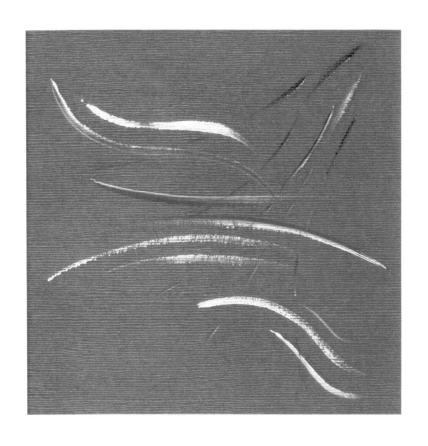

See the wind
like crystal tresses,
combing through
her silvered hair,

Hear the rolling waves
make music,
singing harmonies
with her.

On her body
thin white muslin
lightly covering
radiant flesh,

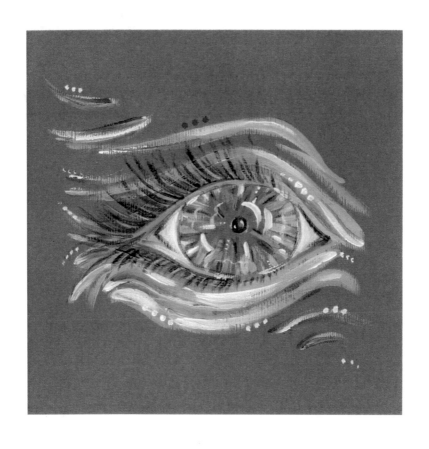

In her eyes
all-knowing fathoms,
iridescent light
and depth.

In her womb

live ancient stories,

safely held

for telling hours,

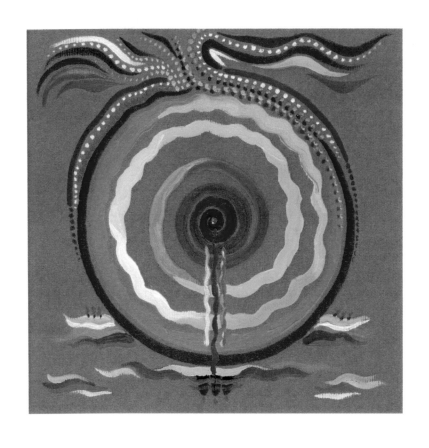

In her breast

a hidden river,

endless source

of reverent power.

See the ground
rise up to meet her
solid footfalls,
open stride,

Feel the arcing lights

above her,
night and day
companion guides.

In her ears

a well of listening,

On her lips

spare wisdom words,

In her smile

all shared belonging,

On her breath

one note still pure.

In her arms

a warm enfolding,

17

On her brow

an eager quest,

In her soul

desire for journey,

Fire for circling

home to rest.

Ride the air

that stirs within her,

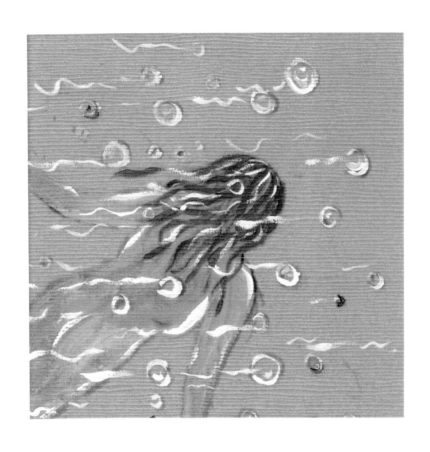

Swim the water

of her ways,

Dance the earth

her joys are seeding,

Tend the flame

she sends each day.

In every generation she passes into holy souls
    and makes them friends of God,
    and prophets.
She reaches mightily from one end of the earth
    to the other,
and she orders all things well.

"And now, my children, listen to me:
    happy are those who keep my ways.
Come, eat of my bread
    and drink of the wine I have mixed."

Wisdom 7: 27, 30b; Proverbs 9:5-6 NRSV

The Ancient One:
She Was, She Is, She Will Be Always

In her hands
she carries nothing,
fingers free,
wide open palms;
On her face
the glow of morning,
night-shade contours
blessing dawn.

On her shoulders
many-colored
woven shawl
of hand-spun yarns;
On her feet
soft woolen slippers,
sturdy fit
for walking far.

See the wind
like crystal tresses,
combing through
her silvered hair;
Hear the rolling
waves make music,
singing harmonies
with her.

On her body
thin white muslin
lightly covering
radiant flesh;
In her eyes
all-knowing fathoms,
iridescent light
and depth.

In her womb
live ancient stories,
safely held
for telling hours;

In her breast
a hidden river,
endless source of
reverent power.

See the ground
rise up to meet her
solid footfalls,
open stride;
Feel the arcing
lights above her,
night and day
companion guides.

In her ears
a well of listening,
On her lips
spare wisdom words;
In her smile
all shared belonging,
On her breath
one note still pure.

In her arms
a warm enfolding,
On her brow
an eager quest;
In her soul
desire for journey,
Fire for circling
home to rest.

Ride the air
that stirs within her,
Swim the water
of her ways,
Dance the earth
her joys are seeding,
Tend the flame
she sends each day.

26

The Ancient One

She Was, She Is, She Will Be Always

Words and Music
Sharon Mick McAuley

In her hands she carries no-thing,
On her bo - dy thin white mus - lin
In her ears a well of lis-tening,

fin - gers free, wide o - pen palms;
light - ly cov - ering ra - diant flesh;
on her lips spare wis-dom words;

on her face the glow of morn-ing,
in her eyes all - know - ing fath-oms,
in her smile all shared be - long-ing,

night - shade con - tours bless-ing dawn.
ir - i - des - cent light and depth.
on her breath one note still pure.

On her shoul - ders man - y col - ored
In her womb live an - cient stor - ies
In her arms a warm en - fold-ing,

wo - ven shawl of hand-spun yarns;
safe - ly held for tel - ling hours;
on her brow an ea - ger quest;

27

The Ancient One

Sharon Mick McAuley

The Vision and The Hope

Just before I leave, we share a big hug. "You coming to see me tomorrow, Gramma?", Caitlyn asks. "Next week, Sweetie," I answer smiling and go out the door as she dances to the window to watch me go down the steps to my car. At two-and-a-half, tomorrow means "soon" to Caitlyn, come again soon.

She signs, "I love you" and blows me a kiss with her whole palm as if she has scooped the kiss off her mouth and is tossing it to me like a ball. She is beaming.

Caitlyn, free little wise one. She is teaching me, bringing me alive like my daughters did. I am laughing more often, and I am quicker to cry. I see things that weren't there before, or were they?

And tomorrow? I believe in it, I trust it because today there is Caitlyn, face shining with a good-bye that is a promise, not an ending.

Little as you are, you can teach me some things:
the world all around us is big,
and high above the world is a blue, blue sky
where the sun, moon and stars all live;
and there is wonder, and there's surprise,
and there is smiling into God's eyes;
there's believing and there is love,
there is seeing in simple trust,
yes there is seeing in simple trust.   29

Little As You Are

Sharon Mick McAuley

Closing Words of Gratitude

1983

For the ways I was brought to life by their birth and the daily gift of their multifaceted beauty that inspires me to awe and gives my life holy meaning, I close with words of gratitude and love for my daughters, Stacey and Erin.

About the Author

Sharon Mick McAuley composed and produced, "River of Life", a collection of sing-a-long songs for Woldumar Nature Center, and "Celtic Prayers to Sing at Dawn and Dusk", 84 melodies for *Sounds of the Eternal: A Celtic Psalter* by J. Philip Newell. Her commissioned cancer-survivor painting, "Sojourn Through the Deep" is on permanent display in the Cancer Care Unit of Hurley Medical Center, and her series, "Jesus: Image of the Invisible God" was completed in 2008 for The Peoples Church in East Lansing.

Sharon's professional ministry has, in this season of her life, distilled into keeping a practice of meditative art making and offering to others spiritual guidance that encourages artistic expression and living in close relationship with God in nature and in community. She believes that a fruitful life of compassion and service to the world flows out of creative authenticity, that is, living 'the image of God'.

Sharon and her husband, Frank, live on a channel of the Grand River in mid-Michigan. She is a native of Michigan with a great love for orchards and lake shores. *The Ancient One* came to her one autumn evening while driving the highway heading up north.